THE HOME GUARD

Neil R. Storey

SHIRE PUBLICATIONS

First published in Great Britain in 2009 by Shire Publications Ltd, Midland House, West Way, Botley, Oxford OX2 0PH, United Kingdom.
44-02 23rd Street, Long Island City, NY 11101, USA.

E-mail: shire@shirebooks.co.uk   www.shirebooks.co.uk

A CIP catalogue record for this book is available from the British Library.

Shire Library no. 574   •   ISBN-13: 978 0 7478 0751 3

Neil Storey has asserted his right under the Copyright, Designs and Patents Act, 1988, to be identified as the author of this book.

Designed by Ken Vail Graphic Design, Cambridge, UK and typeset in Perpetua and Gill Sans.
Printed in China through Worldprint Ltd.

09 10 11 12 13   10 9 8 7 6 5 4 3 2 1

COVER IMAGE
Advancing through a smoke screen at Osterley Park, the first Home Guard training school.

TITLE PAGE IMAGE
Sergeant H. Patient, 19th (Grays) Battalion, Essex Home Guard, October 1944.

CONTENTS PAGE IMAGE
The village of Worstead's local platoon of 5th Battalion, Norfolk Home Guard, 1944.

ACKNOWLEDGEMENTS
I would like to thank: Ron Franklyn; James Hayward; the late Dave Bygrave; Bob Beales; Christine Parmenter; Molly Housego; Tony Smith of Shutters Photographic Studio, Norwich, for studio photography; Nick Wright and all the team at Shire; John Warwicker MBE; Museum of the British Resistance Organisation, Parham, Suffolk; and Robert Bell, Lilian Ream Collection, Wisbech.

Images are acknowledged as follows: Lilian Ream Collection, page 27 (right); Popperfoto/Getty Images, page 32; *Punch*, page 14. IWM images are credited after the captions, with their reference numbers.

All other images were specially commissioned by the author or come from the author's archive.

IMPERIAL WAR MUSEUM COLLECTIONS
Some of the photos in this book come from the Imperial War Museum's collections, which cover all aspects of conflict involving Britain and the Commonwealth since the start of the twentieth century. These resources are available online to search, browse and buy at www.iwmcollections.org.uk You can also visit the Visitor Rooms where you can explore over 8 million photographs, thousands of hours of moving images, the largest sound archive of its kind in the world, thousands of wartime diaries and letters, and a huge reference library. To make an appointment, call (020) 7416 5320, or e-mail mail@iwm.org.uk.
Website: Imperial War Museum www.iwm.org.uk

LIST OF ABBREVIATIONS

AA	Anti-Aircraft
ARP	Air Raid Precautions
BEF	British Expeditionary Force
C-in-C	Commander in Chief
GHQ	General Headquarters
GS(R)	General Staff (Research)
HG	Home Guard
LDV	Local Defence Volunteers
MI(R)	Military Intelligence (Research)
OB	Operation Base
OP	Observation Post
RE	Royal Engineers
WHD	Women's Home Defence
WVS	Women's Voluntary Service

CONTENTS

BRITAIN IN IMMINENT DANGER

THE PURPOSE of this book is to present an overview of the Home Guard, the greatest citizen army Britain has ever seen. Soon after its creation as the Local Defence Volunteers this new army, despite being poorly equipped and having no more than an armband for its uniform, trained and made preparations as best it could to stand against one of the most advanced armies the world had ever seen. Through Britain's darkest hours when invasion appeared imminent it watched and waited. It was only after it was taken under the wing of Churchill that it was re-branded as 'Home Guard'; its organisation, role and training became far more structured, and full uniform, kit and equipment gradually arrived. Comic themes from the 1960s/70s TV series *Dad's Army* can certainly be found, particularly during those early days of its existence in 1940 when invasion was a very real threat. It was a time when the British people stood alone with their 'backs to the wall', and when the need was desperate the shortages of weaponry were at their most acute. This is a story of trials and tribulations, but what was lacking in kit and equipment in 1940 was certainly compensated for with innovation, enthusiasm and uniquely British bold determination.

After seven months of the 'Phoney War', the Battle of France began in earnest on 10 May 1940. Hitler had unleashed his blitzkrieg, and by 14 May German Army Group A had broken through the Ardennes, swept west towards Sedan and had set its sights towards the English Channel. Army Group B had invaded the Netherlands and advanced west through Belgium. The blitzkrieg sped through the continent with such apparent ease that fears of the fall of Belgium, France and Holland left many in no doubt Britain would face the onslaught next. Particular concerns were shown for the use of German paratroops being dropped in advance of any invasion. Some disparate groups of men in towns and villages had already gathered together to discuss how they would defend their homes; they had formed irregular units and had begun patrolling country areas after dark armed with shotguns. In one case in March 1940 Lady Helena Gleichen had become so alarmed at

Opposite:
Fall in! One of the Home Guard platoons from the Dover and Folkestone area assemble for a weekend training exercise, March 1941. (IWM H 8100)

Women of
the Dartmoor
Mounted Patrol
make their final
adjustments before
setting off to keep
their vigil for
enemy paratroops,
August 1940.
(IWM H 2760)

the possibility of German parachute troops landing on the sparsely populated
Herefordshire border with Wales that she organised her staff and tenantry
and even kitted them out with armbands stencilled 'Much Marcle Watchers'.
Nightly patrols began, but due to the shortage of weaponry, she contacted the
battalion headquarters of the King's Shropshire Light Infantry stationed at
Ross-on-Wye to request the loan of eighty rifles, ammunition and 'a couple
of machine guns if you have any'. Such incidents were far from unique. Even
the most sedate of households saw men searching in the back of their desk
drawers for the revolvers they had brought back after their service in the
Great War, and they went out to buy ammunition. Grave conversations were
held in which husbands and wives agreed to keep the last rounds for
themselves. Ex-army officers were also becoming very vocal in the press, on
radio and even on cinema newsreels demanding that they, and many other
like-minded men, be given the chance to volunteer to do something practical
for the defence of their country, even if only to provide suicide squads against
invading forces.

It was fear of the use of paratroops by the enemy that brought matters to
a head. An urgent message was circulated from the Air Ministry to all
commands and repeated to the Admiralty, War Office and Ministry of
Home Security:

Information from Norway shows that German parachute troops, when
descending, hold their arms above their heads as if surrendering.

The parachutist[s], however, hold a grenade in each hand. These are thrown at anyone attempting to obstruct the landing. To counter this strategy, parachutists, if the[y] exceeded six in number, are to be treated as hostile and if possible shot in the air.

Although subsequently this information about the offensive tactics used by the enemy has proved to be erroneous, the deployment of paratroops was very real, and a meeting of senior staff was held on 11 May. Among those who attended were General Sir John Dill, Vice-Chief of the Imperial General Staff, General Sir Robert Gordon-Finlayson and General Sir Walter Kirke. Kirke was well aware of the rising 'martial enthusiasm' in the country and suggested that, if organised properly on a town and village basis, such men in a volunteer defence force could provide a valuable countermeasure against the parachute menace. Further negotiations ran apace regarding the organisation's command structure, how it would be financed and what equipment it would require. Anthony Eden, the newly appointed Secretary of State for War, took a keen interest and secured official Cabinet approval for the formation of the Local Defence Volunteers, an organisation to be placed under Commander-in-Chief (C-in-C) Home Forces. The original idea was for the C-in-C to announce the scheme through a radio broadcast, but Eden wanted to do this personally. Late in the evening of 13 May Eden drafted the broadcast from notes collated by General Kirke, in turn drawn from notes provided by General Gordon-Finlayson. His Majesty's Stationery Office printed thousands of enrolment forms, and telegrams were sent from the Under-Secretary of State at the Home Office to chief constables across the country

'Spot on sight diagram' of a German parachutist. Such illustrations were widely published in newspapers and magazines during the invasion scares of 1940.

Leather covered steel helmet.

Parachute pack.

Web parachute harness.

Sub-calibre machine-gun attached to web belt.

Right hand on release grip of parachute.

Iron rations

Pack.

Gas mask.

Parachute harness

Other men carry grenades, folding cycles, entrenching tools, wireless gear, etc.

arranging the use of police stations as centres where volunteers could present themselves and enrol. Delivery of the necessary forms to police stations was given top priority.

The morning papers of 14 May headlined a 'two thousand tank clash north west of Liege'. Fears over the Fifth Column and spies saw the BBC announce in its German news that any German parachutist found landing in Britain in any kit other than a recognised German uniform would be shot. Holland was swarming with troops, and Queen Wilhelmina had arrived in London as a refugee; that same evening the Dutch Army surrendered. After a brief announcement Anthony Eden broadcast his radio appeal between the 9 o'clock news and a documentary entitled *The Voice of the Nazi*. Eden began:

> I want to speak to you tonight about the form of warfare which the Germans have been employing so extensively against Holland and Belgium – namely the dropping of parachute troops behind the main defensive lines … In order to leave nothing to chance, and to supplement from sources as yet untapped the means of defence already arranged, we are going to ask you to help us in a manner which I know will be welcome to thousands of you. Since the war began the government have received countless inquiries from all over the kingdom from men of all ages who are for one reason or another not at present engaged in military service, and who wish to do something for the defence of their country. Well, now is your opportunity.

Volunteers for the Local Defence Volunteers signing up in the yard of Wimbledon police station, May 1940. (IWM HU 50149)

We want large numbers of such men in Great Britain, who are British subjects, between the ages of seventeen and sixty-five to come forward now and offer their services in order to make assurance doubly sure. The name of the new force which is now to be raised will be the Local Defence Volunteers.

Eden went on to state that the volunteers would be unpaid but they would receive a uniform and would be armed. Those wishing to volunteer were asked to register their names at local police stations. Like a shot from a starting pistol the volunteers poured in, not in hundreds as anticipated but in their thousands through the night and following day; over the country some 250,000 gave their names in the first twenty-four hours.

FORM OF ENROLMENT IN THE LOCAL DEFENCE VOLUNTEERS

Name.. Christian Names ....

Surname First in BLOCK CAPITALS.

QUESTIONS TO BE PUT ON ENROLMENT.

1. What is your name ?
2. What is the date and year of your birth ?
3. What is your address ?
4. (a) Are you a British subject ?
   (b) Nationality of parents at birth ?
   Father
   Mother.
   (c) Name, address and relationship of next of kin
5. Do you now belong to, or have you ever served in the Armed Forces of the Crown ? If so, state particulars of all engagements.
6. Do you understand that if accepted you will become subject to military law and liable to obey such orders as may be given to you in accordance with instructions for the Local Defence Volunteers issued by the Army Council, but that those instructions will require you to give part-time service only and will not require you to live away from home ?
7. Do you understand that your service in the Local Defence Volunteers will be without pay or other emoluments ?
8. Do you understand that in the event of your incurring a disability attributable to your service any claim for compensation will be dealt with under the regulations for the time being in force for the purpose which provide in the case of death or permanent disability the same terms as are applicable to private soldiers and their dependants ?
9. Do you understand that if you are accepted you will engage to serve in the Local Defence Volunteers for a period not exceeding the duration of the present emergency but that during that period your service may be determined in accordance with instructions issued by the Army Council, by competent authority at any time, or at your own request by fourteen days' notice in writing given by you ?

Declaration.

I,..do solemnly declare that the answers made by me to the foregoing questions are true and I hereby agree to serve in the Local Defence Volunteers.

Signature of applicant ....

Date........................ Signature of enrolling authority ....

(Company Commander).

Certificate of Acceptance.

........................(name) is accepted for service in the Local Defence Volunteers for the following period :—
(a) the duration of the emergency
or (b) until........................

Date........................ Signature of accepting authority ....

(Company Commander).

Enrolment form for the Local Defence Volunteers.

LOOK, DUCK AND VANISH

AFTER the place for enrolment into the Local Defence Volunteers (LDV) was announced as the local police station many men set off to join immediately, pausing only to grab their discharge books or put on their medals awarded for service in the First World War; some volunteers arrived at police stations even before the broadcast had ended. Many set out with all due speed with the intention of being the very first to volunteer, only to find a queue had already formed in front of them. So rapid was the response that enrolment forms had not reached every police station, but police officers amicably took down names and addresses. In other areas chief constables sent instructions that each volunteer was to be asked their name and address, whether they were familiar with firearms, their occupation, whether they had any military experience, and whether they were prepared to serve away from home. The police were also given clear instructions that they were not concerned with the administration or control of the LDV, only the registering of the names and addresses of volunteers; however, they were advised to exercise discretion by 'politely sending away' and not recording the names of those clearly too young or too infirm. In addition to those outlined by Mr Eden, the criteria and terms for volunteers were laid down in a War Office circular, which stated the period of service for volunteers would be 'for the duration of the war' and that 'training and duties could be taken in a volunteer's spare time'. There was no medical examination, but men would have to be 'of reasonable physical fitness' and 'capable of free movement'; previous military service and/or a knowledge of firearms (in those days far more country people kept a shotgun to bag a rabbit or pigeon for the pot) were considered advantageous. These points soon evolved into the standard 'Form of Enrolment in the Local Defence Volunteers'. Much to the chagrin of many suitable volunteers already serving in the Air Raid Precautions (ARP) or in the Special Constabulary, they had to be turned down lest the forces they had already been trained in became too depleted. In reality the recruitment terms were flexible; in some small villages men served as both Home Guards (HG) and ARP, or the HG platoon had an ARP duties section.

Opposite:
'Old Contemptibles' in the Local Defence Volunteers lined up for inspection. None of the men pictured wears any official uniform except for the LDV armband. (IWM H 2005)

A commanding officer often used his discretion to enrol enthusiastic youngsters as young as fourteen and fifteen as messengers or volunteers if they looked old enough; some even went so far as to issue the lad with a dispatch rider's army trade badge that many lads wore with great pride as they went speeding off on their bicycles, charged with the delivery of another important message. Discretion was also shown towards old soldiers, especially ex-NCOs over the age limit who had valuable experience to impart – if they were apparently fit enough. There was quite some discussion over who was the oldest serving LDV, the agreed choice being ex-Black Watch Company Sergeant Major Alexander Taylor of Crieff in Scotland, who had served in the Egypt campaign of 1884–5 and was serving in the LDV by special War Office dispensation on his eightieth birthday.

Concurrent with the Eden broadcast, a telegram was sent by Eden to the Lord Lieutenant of every county station, stating, 'I am sure that we may count on your co-operation and help in connection with the Local Defence Volunteer Force.' Each Lord Lieutenant was expected to begin the county structure of the LDV by appointing an area commander with overall command and organisation responsibility for the county. Most entered into the spirit of the request with gusto; some did hesitate, however, and replied with expressions of concern that the men of their county were being invited to become *francs-tireurs* and would thus expose themselves to summary execution if captured by an invading force. Such concerns did not stand long in the face of such enthusiasm among the numbers of volunteers who at least said they wanted to 'do their bit' – whatever the cost.

Each county was divided into zones; some simply used the extant police division areas as frameworks to define their zones. In each zone a headquarters was established to administer the number of groups within it. An unpaid volunteer organiser was to be put in charge of each zone and each group. The numbers involved were not quite like those of the army: whereas a regular army platoon consists of thirty men, the LDV equivalent could range from between ten and fifty men. Most of those appointed to command positions in the LDV had previous military experience, but it was not essential, as those with respected managerial, organisational and leadership skills from civvy street equally found themselves in positions of command. There were also many instances of bosses proudly falling in with all ranks of the LDV; indeed some retired senior officers and NCOs in areas such as Eastbourne (where there were a lot of their kind) were happy to do their bit as private soldiers.

Some factories, railways and the General Post Office arranged their own LDV units. There were also formally organised horse patrols (often raised from local hunts) that operated over moorland, hill country, cliffs and coasts in twenty-four counties. At their height, over nine hundred mounts were

The men and their boats of the Upper Thames Patrol, July 1940. (IWM HU 103328).

The cap badge of the Upper Thames Patrol.

engaged in such work between Cornwall and the Scottish Borders. There were boat patrols upon inland waterways such as the rivers Thames, Trent, Fowey and Fal. In addition to these there were a number of city river patrols, and water patrols on Lake Windermere and the Aire and Calder canal, while later in Norfolk Home Guards served with the Broads Flotilla. One of the first waterborne units was the LDV River Company of the Little Ship Club, which, with its forty boats, patrolled the 19 miles from London Bridge to Teddington. Above Teddington the Upper Thames Patrol, originally formed from the uniformed staff of Thames Conservancy, took over.

Although the War Office announced its intent to issue uniforms of the denim overall type and field service caps, the vast numbers of LDV meant that the uniforms immediately ready for issue did not go far, and uniform for most LDV units in those early weeks and months was almost non-existent. Platoons knew they were coming, but enthusiastically set about drilling and training in their civilian clothes, with the civilian issue gas mask slung and improvised rifle (often a broomstick) carried at the slope on the march. A number of units sought to alleviate their temporary lack of weaponry by seizing school Officers' Training Corps (OTC) rifle armouries 'in the name of the King'. Some such incidents became very heated and required intervention from police and magistrates; formal legal proceedings were instigated in the most extreme cases. Following a public appeal for old weaponry, all manner of firearms and offensive weapons were brought to police stations for use by the LDV. Local museums were also picked over for serviceable weapons and firearms. This brought out some very useable machine guns, pistols and rifles captured during the First World War, but

Local Defence Volunteers drill with broomsticks, May 1940 (IWM MISC_60739).

with them were also impressed ancient and ethnic weaponry of bewildering vintages. For example, a London unit obtained twenty-four cutlasses among a selection of fowling pieces and blunderbusses, which resulted in the creation of a cutlass platoon commanded by an old Royal Navy rating.

The first 'uniform' item to be received by many units in these early days was the 'brassard' – a simple khaki armband printed with the black letters 'LDV'. On 22 May Sir Edward Grigg, the joint parliamentary Under-Secretary of State for War, announced that a quarter of a million armbands were on their way. These supplies were soon consumed, so many variations of the LDV armband were improvised at a local level, screen-printed or embroidered by patriotic local companies or handmade by local Women's Institute (WI) or Women's Voluntary Service (WVS) branches. Eventually the first issue of denim fatigue uniforms arrived with a separate issue of brown leather gaiters. No cap badges were issued. No boots were supplied at this time, and complaints were made about the wear and tear inflicted on the boots of LDV, many of whom sought some compensation for repairs.

The battalion-level ranks of the LDV consisted of battalion commander, company commander and platoon commander, each rank designated with blue stripes on the epaulette (one for platoon, two for company and three for battalion commanders.) Even at this early stage ex-army officers were raiding their army uniforms for their old rank insignia. There soon followed in the NCO corps equivalents of section commander (three chevrons) and squad commander

Above:
Denim overall blouse of a Local Defence Volunteers section commander, May 1940. On the right arm is the 'brassard', the first 'uniform' issued to the LDV.

" I've laid your uniform out, my Lord."

Left: Just one of many cartoon jibes at the LDV for lack of uniform and equipment. *Punch,* 31 July 1940.

A PENGUIN SPECIAL

TOM WINTRINGHAM

NEW WAYS OF WAR

New Ways of War, by Tom Wintringham, published in 1940. From this apparently innocuous Penguin paperback many men of the LDV learned the principles of the art of guerrilla warfare.

(two chevrons). The official title of the ordinary man in the LDV was 'volunteer'.

In these early months of the LDV the training schedules of each battalion varied greatly across the country, but marching drill, training with broomsticks and dummy rifles and what weaponry they had at their disposal at that time began to shape the volunteers into disciplined units. Crucially, the LDV wanted to set to work on the task it had been given. Most zones and groups were rapidly created and their primary function of patrolling set up with duty rotas. Their call-out alarm system was established in the event of an emergency – for most this was to be the ringing of the local church bells; in case this method was prevented by the enemy a 'knock-list' of manual call-outs was usually agreed and often typed out and distributed to the platoon.

The purpose of patrols was to watch the open countryside for enemy paratroops and to either attack swiftly and put the enemy out of action or, if the numbers of enemy were significant and this was not possible, to observe and report any such landings to the local military authorities; hence the nickname of 'the Look, Duck and Vanish Brigade' did, in fact, state their primary function. Next they were expected to 'pin down' the enemy with fire or impede and frustrate the advance of any such enemy incursions, but with only minimal weaponry, what were they to do? Throughout 1940 there was also a real fear of the 'Fifth Column', a covert organisation of German operatives and British citizens turned collaborators already in the county that could rise up at any minute and attack utilities and railways to cause maximum disruption and a pre-emptive strike before a main invasion attempt. To counter this threat a number of LDV had to spend many a cold dark night out in the wilds with little shelter or comfort, manning improvised roadblocks or guarding important sites such as railway bridges, goods sidings, waterworks or electricity generating stations, often making themselves unpopular by demanding to examine identity cards from people (including police officers) who were not aware the LDV were entitled to do so and were willing to argue the point.

Faced with limited supplies of weaponry, but still wanting to counter the threat of any potential invader or Fifth Columnist, the answer was to train the men in unarmed combat. Many platoons were filled with experienced ex-soldiers, but the most up-to-date experiences of warfare came from those who had served in the International Brigade during the Spanish Civil War.

Most LDV units learned the latest guerrilla warfare tactics, methods of hand-to-hand combat and street fighting from books and magazine articles written by such experienced fighters as Tom Wintringham, author of *New Ways of War* (1940), whose features on the subject also appeared in the magazine *Picture Post*. Working from the books or magazines, the LDV would be given lectures and practical demonstrations by their officers and NCOs, which they would then practise. Training in unarmed combat was certainly greeted with gusto – although it was marked by an increase in sales of sticking plasters and liniment when the sessions were staged.

In those early days the *Dad's Army* image of the LDV was established. Despite great strides and achievements in the standard of efficiency and training, as the war progressed the old stigma lingered on, as did scathing nicknames played on the letters 'LDV' worn on the armband of every volunteer: 'Long Dentured Veterans', 'Last Ditch Volunteers' and the one that stuck, 'the Look, Duck and Vanish Brigade'.

Members of the Local Defence Volunteers being taught simple German phrases. (IWM HU 50154)

Punch

SUMMER NUMBER

1/-

BEATING THE INVADER

Between 26 May and 4 June 1940 the beleaguered British Expeditionary Force (BEF) was evacuated from the beaches of Dunkirk in Operation *Dynamo*, an evacuation made more poignant and undaunted by J. B. Priestly in his Postscript to the News 'Little Ships' broadcast of 5 June 1940. Dunkirk was not just an evacuation, but it heralded a defeat for the BEF. On 18 June Churchill grimly announced in Parliament:

> What General Weygand called the Battle of France is over. I expect that the Battle of Britain is about to begin. Upon this battle depends the survival of Christian civilisation. Upon it depends our own British life, and the long continuity of our institutions and our Empire. The whole fury and might of the enemy must very soon be turned on us.

By the time France capitulated on 25 June, many British households had already received the 'If the Invader Comes' leaflet. The leaflet advised the civilian population to 'stay put', look out for and report suspicious activity, and help British troops and LDV if ordered to do so. It outlined the precautions to take that would enable people not to help the enemy, such as hiding maps and immobilising vehicles, and suggested if one owned a factory to organise its defence 'at once'.

July 1940 proved to be a turning point for the LDV. George Child-Villiers, 9th Earl of Jersey, a friend of Lord Hulton, the influential owner of *Picture Post*, gave permission for his grounds at Osterley Park, Hounslow, West London, to become the first LDV training school. The project was predominantly financed by Hulton (who was also organising a private supply of weapons from the United States), while Tom Wintringham was the key player in the practical creation of the school, and took the role of its director of training. The school was certainly an irregular one, at least in the experience of military training establishments to date. No drill or square bashing was conducted there; within twenty minutes of arrival students were down to hands-on practical training. Wintringham's lecturers taught the

Opposite:
Mr Punch and his P.17 rifle (note the red band) on the cover of the *Punch* summer number, 1942.

Members of Norfolk Home Guard defend their roadblock against an enemy 'tank' at the coastal town of Sheringham, 1940.

theory and practice of modern mechanical and guerrilla warfare using the estate workers' homes – then scheduled for demolition – as a battle school for street-fighting techniques; Wintringham even brought over some Basque explosives experts he had encountered during the Spanish Civil War to impart their knowledge. Lecturers included Stanley White, one of the chief instructors of the Boy Scouts' Association, a man who had learned his scouting skills from Baden-Powell personally; Hugh Slater acted as modern warfare tactics expert; the English surrealist painter Roland Penrose taught practical camouflage techniques; Major Wilfred Vernon gave instruction in the art of making Molotov cocktails and mixing homemade explosives; and Canadian Bert 'Yank' Levy, who had served under Wintringham in the Spanish Civil War, taught knife fighting and hand-to-hand combat. In the first three months of its existence over 5,000 volunteers passed through Osterley Park. Indeed the lines upon which the training centre was established and run proved to be a model for three further training schools that were set up in other locations across the country. Curiously, since Wintringham and his men had fought for the communists in Spain, concerns were raised by the British security services that he might be training those who passed through Osterley Park in methods of guerrilla warfare that could be used against the government. After just three months and with interest from the press from both sides of the Atlantic,

Far left: *Manual of Guerilla Tactics*, one of a number of advanced training guides published by Bernards (Publishers) Ltd.

Left: *Home Guard Manual of Camouflage* by English surrealist artist Roland Penrose – one of the original team of instructors at Osterley Park.

Below: *If the Invader Comes*, the government leaflet sent to every British household in June 1940.

Osterley Park was taken over by the military, and Wintringham and his 'communist' lecturers were pushed aside. Others such as Roland Penrose were drafted to the new War Office School for Instructors to the Home Guard.

On 23 July 1940 Winston Churchill, who had never liked the cumbersome and somewhat ridiculed title of Local Defence Volunteers, saw it formally announced that the organisation be renamed Home Guard (HG). This was not only a change in name but also ushered in a new raft of improvements: structured training, uniform and weaponry supplies and official recognition were set in motion for the million HGs across the country.

Churchill also appealed to the United States for the first major issue of rifles for HGs. His call was answered with a batch of Canadian Ross rifles and by far the larger issue of half a million P.14 and P.17 Springfield rifles, all of First World War vintage. These came in thick paraffin grease, and many platoon histories record the sterling work of women volunteers and the likes of local WVS who helped to clean the weapons up, but ammunition and issue

Issued by the Ministry of Information in co-operation with the War Office and the Ministry of Home Security.

If the
INVADER
comes

WHAT TO DO — AND HOW TO DO IT

THE Germans threaten to invade Great Britain. If they do so they will be driven out by our Navy, our Army and our Air Force. Yet the ordinary men and women of the civilian population will also have their part to play. Hitler's invasions of Poland, Holland and Belgium were greatly helped by the fact that the civilian population was taken by surprise. They did not know what to do when the moment came. *You must not be taken by surprise.* This leaflet tells you what general line you should take. More detailed instructions will be given you when the danger comes nearer. Meanwhile, read these instructions carefully and, be prepared to carry them out.

I

When Holland and Belgium were invaded, the civilian population fled from their homes. They crowded on the roads, in cars, in carts, on bicycles and on foot, and so helped the enemy by preventing their own armies from advancing against the invaders. You must not allow that to happen here. Your first rule, therefore, is —

(1) IF THE GERMANS COME, BY PARACHUTE, AEROPLANE OR SHIP, YOU MUST REMAIN WHERE YOU ARE. THE ORDER IS "STAY PUT".

If the Commander in Chief decides that the place where you live must be evacuated, he will tell you when and how to leave. Until you

receive such orders you must remain where you are. If you run away, you will be exposed to far greater danger because you will be machine-gunned from the air as were civilians in Holland and Belgium, and you will also block the roads by which our own armies will advance to turn the Germans out.

II

There is another method which the Germans adopt in their invasion. They make use of the civilian population in order to create confusion and panic. They spread false rumours and issue false instructions. In order to prevent this, you should obey the second rule, which is as follows :—

(2) DO NOT BELIEVE RUMOURS AND DO NOT SPREAD THEM. WHEN YOU RECEIVE AN ORDER, MAKE QUITE SURE THAT IT IS A TRUE ORDER AND NOT A FAKED ORDER. MOST OF YOU KNOW YOUR POLICEMEN AND YOUR A.R.P. WARDENS BY SIGHT, YOU CAN TRUST THEM. IF YOU KEEP YOUR HEADS, YOU CAN ALSO TELL WHETHER A MILITARY OFFICER IS REALLY BRITISH OR ONLY PRETENDING TO BE SO. IF IN DOUBT ASK THE POLICEMAN OR THE A.R.P. WARDEN. USE YOUR COMMON SENSE.

A selection of Home Guard cap badges: (a) The Cambridgeshire Regiment were delivered a batch of misspelt cap badges with no 'e' – these were refused by the men of the regiment and issued instead to many of the Cambridgeshire Home Guard battalions. Two of the cap badges made specifically for Home Guard battalions in Rutland (b) and Huntingdonshire (c). Factory Home Guard units often had their own badges; this example (d) was worn by members of the 1st Battalion, Vickers Armaments Home Guard.

cleaning materials for rifle maintenance were still in short supply. The rifle itself had an awkward action in comparison to the Lee Enfield of the Great War. The problem with the P.17 was that it fired .300 ammunition – not the standard British Army .303 – so a red band was painted around the barrel of this rifle to avoid ammunition confusion. However, despite these setbacks HGs agreed these rifles were better than the hotchpotch of weaponry they had before.

One great move in the wake of the new changes was on 3 August 1940, when the Home Guard was affiliated to its county regiments and was granted permission to wear the regimental cap badge and the woollen worsted battledress of its regular and territorial army counterparts (some HG units did, however, opt to wear their own badge). Battledress was adorned with a khaki cloth shoulder title with the words 'Home Guard' printed upon it in yellow (some areas did adopt a colour-coded lettering but yellow was standard). Beneath the shoulder title would be letter designations for the county, with the battalion number beside or below it. The county designations were as shown opposite.

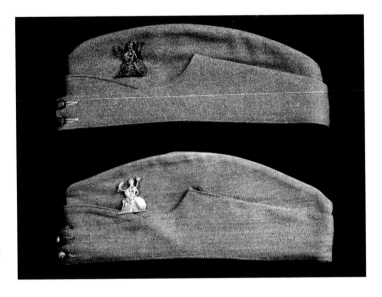

Two types of FS (Field Service) caps worn by Norfolk Home Guard: the officer's version (top), privately purchased from a military tailor, was made in barathea with bronze buttons and regimental cap badge; the version for NCOs and other ranks (bottom) was issued and made in worsted barathea with brass buttons and regimental cap badge. Other counties would have the same type of hats but wore cap badges relevant to them.

A	Anglesey	ER	East Riding of	NN	Northamptonshire
AB	Aberdeenshire and		Yorkshire	NRY	North Riding of
	City of Aberdeen	ESX	Essex		Yorkshire
ABK	Aberdeenshire	F	Fife	NS	North Staffordshire
	(Kincardineshire Bn)	F&D	Denbighshire	NTS	Nottinghamshire
ANG	Angus		(Denbigh/Flint Bn)	ORK	Orkney
ARG	Argyllshire	FT	Flintshire	OXF	Oxfordshire
AYR	Ayrshire	G	City of Glasgow	PEM	Pembrokeshire
BDF	Bedfordshire	GLN	Glamorganshire	R	Ross-shire
BHM	Warwickshire	GLS	Gloucestershire	R&B	Renfrewshire and
	(Birmingham)	H	Hampshire and Isle of		Buteshire Bn
BNF	Banffshire		Wight	REN	Renfrewshire
BR	Brecknockshire	HD	Lincolnshire	R-L	Ross-shire (Lewis Bn)
BRX	Berkshire		(Holland)	RR	Radnorshire
BUX	Buckinghamshire	HDS	Huntingdonshire	RU	Rutland
CA	Caithness	HFD	Herefordshire	SB	Scottish Border
CAM	Cambridgeshire	HTS	Hertfordshire	SF	Derbyshire
CC	Caernarvonshire	IOM	Isle of Man	SFK	Suffolk
CDN	Cardiganshire	IN	Inverness-shire	SHR	Shropshire
CH	Cheshire		(Nairnshire Bn)	SKR	Stewartry of
CLN	Clackmannanshire	INV	Inverness-shire		Kirkcudbrightshire
CO	Cornwall	K	Lincolnshire	SOM	Somerset
COL	City of London		(Kesteven)	SS	South Staffordshire
COV	Warwickshire	KT	Kent	STG	Stirlingshire
	(Coventry)	L	Lincolnshire (Lindsey)	SU	Sutherland
CRM	Carmarthenshire	LEI	Leicestershire	SX	Sussex
CT	Lincolnshire (Lincoln	LF	Lancashire (21, 22,	SY	Surrey
	– County Town)		27, 41–3, 55, 60 and	TAY	Perthshire
CUM	Cumberland		64 Bns)	TWD	Peeblesshire
DBT	Dumbartonshire	LK	Lanarkshire	UTP	Upper Thames Patrol
DDE	City of Dundee	LON	County of London	WAR	Warwickshire
DEN	Denbighshire	LR	Lancashire	WES	Westmorland
DFS	Dumfriesshire	M	Merioneth and	WL	West Lancashire
DHM	Durham		Montgomery	WL	West Lothian
DOR	Dorset	MAN	Lancashire (23, 25,	WNM	Wigtownshire
DVN	Devon		26, 44–51, 56, 61		(Machars Bn)
EHG	City of Edinburgh		and 63 Bns)	WNR	Wigtownshire
EL	Lancashire (1–15,	ML	Midlothian		(Rhinns Bn)
	28–32, 57–9 and	MON	Monmouthshire	WOR	Worcestershire
	62 Bns)	MRY	Moray	WR	West Riding of
EL	East Lothian	MX	Middlesex		Yorkshire
ELY	Isle of Ely	ND	Northumberland	WTS	Wiltshire
		NK	Norfolk	Z	Zetland

23

Above:
The side-by-side method of wearing battalion and county designations on an officer's tunic from 14th (Hapton) Battalion, Norfolk Home Guard. Note the standard Home Guard worsted backed lieutenant's pips on the epaulette.

Above right:
The above and below county and battalion designations on a sergeant's tunic from 2nd (Hitchin) Battalion, Hertfordshire Home Guard.

Although official HMSO training manuals were certainly used by HG units, it was only in September 1940 that *Home Guard: A Handbook for the LDV* by John Brophy was published. Adopted as the Home Guard *vade mecum*, this book went through numerous reprints and no fewer than eleven revised editions between 1940 and 1942 and was finally entitled *The Home Guard Handbook*. It proved to be the first of a number of HG training manuals penned by Brophy. His next book standardised the drill commands and parade ground discipline across the country, as some old NCOs were insisting on using the old drill of the Great War, others using 1930s drill books; thus *A Home Guard Drill Book and Field Service Manual* was produced by Brophy in November 1940.

The training manuals gave a number of helpful tips for improvised anti-tank warfare. After explaining how the enemy tank driver's view is limited to slot sights when the lid is closed, the manual explains:

a sheet is disguised to resemble the ground in a narrow lane. On either side of the lane is a man and when the vehicle is about to pass them they each drag on a piece of rope or wire running through the edge of the sheet and passing over tree branches of gate posts. The sheet rises from the ground and before the tank can stop it is completely enveloped and blinded.

The unworn insignia, spare buttons, 'Mons' Star trio medal ribbon, cap badge and other contents of the sewing kit belonging to a corporal in 31st (Smethwick) Battalion, South Staffordshire Home Guard.

The driver would have to stop or risk an accident; thus cloaked, the other waiting 'tank busters' of the HG detachment could then rapidly move in, ramming a crowbar between the track and wheel, then prising it off or blowing it off with an improvised tank charge (4–6 pounds of plastic explosive with a Bickford fuse and detonator sheathed in a cocoa tin), consequently disabling the tank. It is then a sitting duck for the HG's 'Molotovs' (petrol bombs). Three of these strategically placed on the tank could lead to the fire being taken into the tank's air intake, causing it to 'brew up' (set on fire).

Another guide suggests that a plentiful supply of metal plates with their undersides painted black could be laid across a narrow entrance roadway

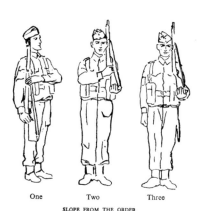

One   Two   Three

SLOPE FROM THE ORDER

Bottom left: Rifle drill illustration from *A Home Guard Drill Book and Field Service Manual*, by John Brophy, published in November 1940.

Bottom right: Published in September 1940, *Home Guard: A Handbook for the LDV* was the first of a number of training manuals by John Brophy written specifically for and adopted by the Home Guard.

Members of the West Riding Home Guard attacking an enemy 'tank' with 'Molotovs' during a training exercise, Doncaster, October 1940. (IWM H 4763)

into a village to give the impression of anti-tank mines. A little straw scattered over them could look like some attempt to hide them. The enemy tank commander stops, opens his hatch to investigate and lo! the waiting HGs in the two-storey house above him send down a few Molotovs – into the hatch of his tank! Armed with such inspiring methods of improvised anti-tank warfare, most Home Guard companies trained as per these instructions, and most of them established their own anti-tank platoons.

By winter 1940 most HGs at least had access to a greatcoat and tin helmet for their patrol duties. By early 1941 most units were fully uniformed

The weapons of the tank buster – a crate containing 'Molotov' cocktails, some petrol and a funnel to fill more, two types of 'Jam Tin' bombs and a cocoa powder tin containing a 4-pound charge of plastic explosive to blow off a tank track.

Above:
Sergeant's battledress blouse from 4th (Pocklington)
Battalion, East Riding Home Guard. Displayed on
it is the standard Home Guard webbing kit of BAR
(Browning Automatic Rifle) pouches, cross straps and
a leather belt, from which is worn a P.14 bayonet and
scabbard attached by a brown leather frog. The cross
straps were fastened at the back with a pair of buckles
on a webbing attachment that slid onto the belt.

Right:
A sergeant in Lincolnshire Home Guard wearing
standard Home Guard webbing. His service
respirator bag is slung from his right shoulder to
his left side; in his right hand is a P.14 rifle. Note
his leather gaiters; usually brown leather, these
were fastened by leather tabs and brass buckles
and were distinctive of the Home Guard uniform.

and even had issue boots. A checklist leaflet was soon issued, stipulating 'What you must do when the Home Guard is Mustered':

> Put on uniform and take the whole of your Arms and Equipment to the place where you have been instructed to report.
>
> Bring the undermentioned articles with you, but no *superfluous* ones:
>
> a) Enough food to last 24 hours, drinking mug and plate or mess tin, with knife, fork and spoon.
>
> b) Razor, lather brush, hairbrush and comb, towel, soap and toilet paper.
>
> c) Change of underclothing, spare pair of socks, handkerchiefs. Have a rucksack or sandbag ready to hold the above.
>
> d) One blanket rolled bandolier fashion.
>
> e) Spade or pick if you have them.
>
> f) Identity card bearing battalion stamp.
>
> g) All your own Ration Books.
>
> h) Envelopes, notepaper and pen or pencil.
>
> i) Tobacco and/or cigarettes.
>
> j) Matches and/or torch.
>
> k) Spare pair of bootlaces.

The contents of a Home Guard haversack – with a few private purchase additions for the more senior soldier.

On 1 February 1941 the War Office sanctioned full commissions to Home Guard officers, and the old blue stripes of the LDV ranks were replaced with

the full military system, such as cloth crown and pips with plain khaki backing for officers and chevrons for NCOs. The rank system equated thus: Zone Commander (Brigadier), Group Commander (Colonel), Battalion Commander (Lieutenant Colonel), Company Commander (Major), Platoon Commander (Captain or Lieutenant), Section Commander (Sergeant), Squad Commander (Corporal or Lance Corporal). Volunteers remained so by name until November 1941, when conscription was introduced to ensure the Home Guard was kept up to strength. Each man was expected to attend up to forty-eight hours' training or guard duties a month or face a penalty of a £10 fine or a month in prison. Thus the volunteer character of the Home Guard finally disappeared and volunteers became privates.

Devon Home Guard Motorcycle Messengers c. 1942. On the upper arm each man wears white and blue signals armbands as an identifying mark of his duties.

The year 1941 also saw the introduction of two significant new branches of the Home Guard. In May 1941 authority was granted for the formation of HG motor coach and transport companies. The need for troop- and load-carrying vehicles to ferry ammunition, regular army and HGs was clear, but it took quite some time for the units to evolve from their existing battalions. The first to be approved was 59 (Taxi) Battalion, County of London, on 6 August. By the end of the year four units formed in London had mustered some 1,200 taxis and 480 lorries, plus numerous control cars and motorcycles. Many more such units followed across the country.

Insignia of the London Home Guard Motor Transport Companies.

The second significant development came with the establishment of the first Home Guard bomb disposal squads in June. Limited to factory HG units, their duties were confined to the factory or premises of their unit, but the most highly trained units could be asked to volunteer for duties outside. The units had three classes. Category 'A' units were highly trained

Factory Defence, the guide to factory defence strategies, by Colonel G. A. Wade, MC.

FACTORY DEFENCE
by COL. G. A. WADE, M.C.
Author of 'The Defence of Bloodford Village' etc.

THE GALE & POLDEN TRAINING SERIES
Price 1/6 net. by post 1/8

Badge of Home Guard Bomb Disposal Sub-Unit members who had performed twenty-four hours' bomb disposal training. The first issue of ten thousand of these badges was made in August 1943.

and authorised to work on bombs, including the discharging and removal of certain types of fuses without Royal Engineer (RE) Bomb Disposal supervision. Category 'B' were able to carry out the same duties as 'A' category men, but required RE supervision for fuse-discharging and removal. Category 'C' units were still undergoing training. By 1943 Home Guard Auxiliary Bomb Disposal sub-units could be found in factories as diverse as Hawker Aircraft in Kingston-upon-Thames and Chivers, the jam manufacturers in Cambridge.

The Home Guard maintained their dusk till dawn patrols long after the immediate threat of invasion had passed. Evening watch was usually set from 9.30 p.m. to 1.30 a.m., then change of guard for dawn watch from 1.30 a.m. to 5.30 a.m. Many of these men would then have to do a day's work, although the retired 'old boys' often took the dawn watch so the younger, working men could get a good night's sleep. After the initial issue of rifles in 1940/41, a piecemeal trickle turned into a considerable flow of weaponry dispatched to the Home Guard: bayonets arrived for the rifles; Thompson sub-machine guns and Browning automatic rifles appeared in most platoons; and companies often had the likes of Lewis or Vickers machine guns. Thompsons were later recalled from HG units and issued to commandos; the gap in the HG armoury was later filled by an issue of Sten guns. The first weapon received by anti-tank sections was the Blacker Bombard (later re-titled 'Spigot Mortar'), devised by Lieutenant Colonel Stewart Blacker in the early years of the Second World War. Although intended for use by the regular units of the British Army, it was quickly replaced by the PIAT (Projector, Infantry, Anti-tank) and was issued to the Home Guard instead. This was a cumbersome weapon: the three-man crew could deploy the weapon to be fired from the ground on its portable mountings, or it could be mounted on one of the many concrete spigot mortar mount emplacements fixed at defensive points across the country. The anti-tank round for this weapon was a 20-pound finned bomb full of high explosive, propelled by a black powder charge sufficient to give it a range of over 100 yards, albeit with a curved trajectory.

Above:
A typical 'Tommy gun' issued to Home Guard units. Properly known as the Thompson sub-machine gun M1928, this example has Lyman adjustable sights, a Cutts Compensator and 50-round .45 Calibre SMG drum magazine.

Left:
The *Tommy Gun, Rifle and Bayonet* manual published by Nicholson & Watson, *c*.1941.

Below:
The Sten Mk II sub-machine gun, issued to the Home Guard after most Tommy guns were withdrawn for re-issue to regular army troops. Upon seeing the cheaply produced Sten, one HG recalled: 'I knew we were going to win the war. "At last," I thought, "we've ditched the fine British craftsmanship nonsense."'

Members of
the 25th County
of London
(Blackheath)
Battalion on
a camouflaged
exercise with their
Spigot Mortar in
the foreground.

Major Northover
demonstrating his
projector; this
version was built
on a wheeled
carriage for
easier transport.
(IWM H 12679)

Against German tank designs of the early part of the war such a warhead would have been quite effective. There was also an anti-personnel round that weighed 14 pounds and could be fired out to 500 yards, but it remained an unpopular weapon.

Anti-tank sections were much happier with the arrival of Northover Projectors, designed by Major Robert Harry Northover specifically for use by the Home Guard. Northover travelled around the country personally demonstrating his weapon at training events. In effect the Northover was a drainpipe with a breech standing on a tripod; it was the last black powder weapon used by the British Army. It required a crew of three: a gunner and a loader would have sufficed, but as it was very heavy (the projector itself weighed about 60 pounds, the base plate and legs about 74 pounds) so rapid movement with the weapon was only possible with three men.

A Northover could fire a Self-Igniting Phosphorous (SIP) bomb (otherwise known as the Albright and Wilson or AW Bomb) several hundred yards onto an enemy tank. Upon impact the bomb's glass casing would shatter and the benzene and phosphor ignite, cloaking the enemy armoured vehicle in clouds of thick smoke. The Northover was then capable of firing an anti-tank (AT)

Above:
Manual of the Northover Projector, the last black powder weapon used by British forces.

A Northover projector and crew, c. 1942.

A Smith gun and crew, c. 1942.

grenade, or a bombing party could move in on the tank with Molotovs or charges. A lighter Mk II version was devised and introduced later in the war, but for distance transport it was advisable to mount it on a wheeled carriage.

The Home Guard even had its own 'field gun'. Developed in 1940 as an emergency gun for the Home Guard, the Smith Gun was the product of a private venture by the chief engineer of the Trianco Engineering Company, Sheffield (renowned for its heating appliances). It consisted of a 3-inch smoothbore barrel designed to fire a 3-inch mortar shell, and it was mounted on a light gun carriage. There was also a limber for extra ammunition, all of which was light enough to be towed by an ordinary motor car. When deployed the carriage was simply upended onto one of its wheels and was ready for action. Most HGs thought the Smith gun looked more like an overgrown product from the Tri-ang toy company. For each new weapon training would be given and proficiency examinations staged. Soon a certificate and proficiency badge were established for passing proficiency tests in six areas of Home Guard skills, such as general HG knowledge, rifle, 36 Mills grenade, signalling, battlecraft and map reading. The badge for proficiency passed in six areas was denoted by a square of red felt worn in the form of a diamond on the right forearm of the battledress tunic 5 inches from the bottom of the sleeve. As more weaponry came through for HGs, further tests were initiated and an additional proficiency badge in the form of an oblong was introduced to be worn under the red diamond. Accordingly, further training guides were produced and John Brophy's previous volumes were accompanied by his

Above:
Home Guard proficiency badges were initially worn on the lower right sleeve until May/June 1944, when they were moved to the lower left to allow space for war service chevrons.

Right:
Home Guard Certificate of Proficiency awarded to Private W. R. Litchfield, D Company, 9th (Brixworth) Battalion, Northamptonshire Home Guard.

A.F.W 4026.

Certificate of Proficiency
HOME GUARD

On arrival at the Training Establishment, Primary Training Centre or Recruit Training Centre, the holder must produce this Certificate at once for the officer commanding, together with Certificate A if gained in the Junior Training Corps or Army Cadet Force.

PART I. I hereby certify that (Rank) Pte. (Name and initials) LITCHFIELD, W.R.
of "D" Battery 9th N.N. Regiment HOME GUARD has qualified Company Battalion
in the Proficiency Badge tests as laid down in the pamphlet "Qualifications for, and Conditions governing the Award of the Home Guard Proficiency Badges and Certificates" for the following subjects :—

Subject	Date	Initials
1. General knowledge (all candidates)		
2. Rifle	9.2.44	ceo.
3. 36 M Grenade	9.2.44	ceo.
4. (a) Other weapon STEN GUN	9.2.44	ceo
(b) Signalling	14.3.44	ceo
5. (a) Battlecraft, (b) Coast Artillery, (c) Heavy A.A. Bty. work, (d) "Z" A.A. Battery work, (e) Bomb Disposal, (f) Watermanship, (g) M.T.		
6. (a) Map Reading, (b) Field works, (c) First Aid	18.3.44	ceo
	18.3.44	ceo

Date 9th February, 1944 Signature .... * President or Member of the Board.

Date 15 MAR 1944 194— Signature .... * President or Member of the Board.

Date 194— Signature .... * President or Member of the Board.

Date 194— Signature .... * President or Member of the Board.

Date 194— Signature .... * President or Member of the Board.

PART II. I certify that (Rank) Pte. (Name and initials) LITCHFIELD, W.R.
of 'D' Battery 9 Northants.HG Regiment HOME GUARD, having duly passed Company Battalion
the Proficiency tests in the subjects detailed above in accordance with the pamphlet and is hereby authorized to wear the Proficiency Badge as laid down in Regulations for the Home Guard, Vol. I, 1942, para. 41d.

Date 29th March, 1944 Signature .... Lt.Col.
Commanding 9 Northants. Bn. H.G.

PART III. If the holder joins H.M. Forces, his Company or equivalent Commander will record below any particulars which he considers useful in assessing the man's value on arrival at the T.E., P.T.C., R.T.C., e.g. service, rank, duties on which employed, power of leadership, etc.

Date 194— Signature .... O.C.
where not applicable.

HOME GUARD PROFICIENCY
By
JOHN BROPHY

100 PRACTICAL QUESTIONS — WITH ANSWERS : PROBLEMS OF STRATEGY AND TACTICS : THE NORTHOVER : THE S.T. GRENADE : THE "THERMOS" ANTI-TANK GRENADE : GERMAN RIFLES, SUB-MACHINE GUNS, AUTOMATIC PISTOLS, HAND GRENADES

DIAGRAMS AND DETAILS. 124 PAGES

HODDER & STOUGHTON LIMITED 1/6 net

Left:
John Brophy's *Home Guard Proficiency* (1942).

Right:
Bradford Home Guard proficiency badge – a rare and possibly unique example of an area producing its own proficiency badges.

35

The answer to invasion – Ju-Jitsu!

YOUR ANSWER TO INVASION JU-JITSU

UNARMED COMBAT

The Art of Physical Defence and Attack
practically explained and illustrated by

JAMES HIPKISS
(British Ju-Jitsu Champion)
INCLUDING A SPECIAL CONCISE COURSE FOR INSTRUCTORS

2/-

Insignia of 103 AA Rocket Battery, County of London Home Guard (Southwark Park) with Anti-Aircraft Command formation sign below, 1943.

Advanced Training for Home Guards (June 1941), soon followed by Roland Penrose's *Home Guard Manual of Camouflage* (October 1941) and Brophy's *Home Guard Proficiency* (1942).

As training became more standardised and far more organised, HG training programmes show evenings dedicated to drill, weapons proficiency, gas recognition and protection, first aid, use of cover, camouflage and concealment. There were practices for weekend exercises and competitions at regional and district level, with cups and shields awarded for the likes of bombing, bayonet fighting, field craft, squad and small arms drill, stretcher bearing and musketry. More guidebooks were also produced as training aids. Gale and Polden created a variety of guidebooks for soldiers on a wide range of subjects from patrolling and stalking to self-defence. Bernards (Publishers) Ltd of London produced some of the more specialist guides to guerrilla tactics, explosives, weaponry, radios and enemy recognition. A variety of publishers went on to offer a wide range of similar titles, among them *Your Answer to Invasion – Ju-Jitsu*, by James Hipkiss (1941); *All in Fighting*, by Captain W. E. Fairbairn of Fairbairn-Sykes fighting knife fame (1943); *Harrying the Hun: A Handbook of Scouting, Stalking and Camouflage*, by Norman Demuth (*c.* 1943) and *Unarmed Action: A Handbook for the Home Guard*, by Micky Wood, lightweight wrestling champion of Great Britain (1943).

With the drafting of fifty thousand regular artillerymen overseas in September 1941, a trial was set up in Liverpool with the Home Guard manning one of the new and still listed secret anti-aircraft (AA) rocket batteries; they were codenamed 'Z' Batteries. The trial proved to be very successful, and in December 1941 the War Office announced HG personnel were to be 'employed on certain duties in AA Command'. To ensure war production and home life would not suffer unduly from the demands of war, a government ruling stipulated no HG engaged in such work should exceed forty-eight hours' training and duty in any twenty-eight-day period. The single barrel projector was the main weapon; with sixty-four of these grouped in one location each site required 178 HG for every nightly duty. In a week with eight shifts just over 1,400 men were required for every HG rocket site. Initially no new HG battalions were to be formed for these duties, but this changed in March 1942 when the new batteries were reorganised into independent HG units. In June 1942 these batteries were given county designations in accordance with the county in which they were formed, and numbered sequentially, commencing with 101; half an inch below this was worn the AA formation patch of the parent AA division (replaced by the new formation sign worn by all troops in AA command in January 1943). Despite the enthusiastic reception, the scheme initially generated just seven thousand HG volunteers. Men brought into the HG as conscripts were assigned to the 'Z' Batteries but proved unreliable at turning up. In October 1942 some heavy AA battery duties were also passed to Home Guard units, and artillery gunners were replaced along the coast at many locations with 'emergency batteries' manned by the Home Guard. Still the pressure was on to find men for both rockets and heavy AA, so with no other option open to them in 1943 authorities introduced the unpopular compulsory transfer of HGs to gunner duties.

A rocket battery manned by members of the Home Guard. (IWM H 16371)

I have received The King's command to express His Majesty's appreciation of the loyal service given voluntarily to her country in a time of grievous danger by

MRS. E.M.DALTON

as a Woman Home Guard Auxiliary.

The War Office,
London.

Secretary of State
for War

Above:
A Suffolk Women's Home Guard auxiliary 1943–4.

Top right:
(upper) Women's Home Defence badge.
(lower) The plastic Women's HG Auxiliary badge.

Right:
A certificate of thanks to Mrs E. M. Dalton. Women auxiliaries were also permitted to keep their badges.

The Home Guard had reached its peak strength at the end of 1942, with 1,850,757 serving in all ranks. Officially, there was not a woman among them. Unofficially, women had been trained in the firing of rifles and had been helping run the administration of HG units since they began. Dissatisfied with the situation, Dr Edith Summerskill, Labour MP for Fulham West, raised the matter of women serving in the HG but was simply rebuffed; after joining forces with champion shot Marjorie Foster, they established an organisation known as Women's Home Defence (WHD). The number of women in WHD rapidly grew to twenty thousand serving in 250 units. The War Office could no longer ignore the sheer weight of numbers involved in this unofficial unit, and in April 1943 women were permitted to enter the ranks of the HG, nominated as official auxiliaries with duties restricted to secretarial, telephone, catering or transport duties. The old concerns first voiced over the creation of the LDV reared up again, and consideration had to be given to how these women could be protected from being summarily shot as *franc tireurs* in the event of an invasion. The answer was a protection certificate endorsed with their unit stamp, which stated the holder's name and their employment in the HG, and pointed out that the bearer 'is authorised to follow the Armed Forces of the Crown and is entitled in the event of capture by the enemy to be treated as a prisoner of war'. By September 1944 32,000 women were serving with the Home Guard.

Hampshire Home Guard officers and Women Home Guard auxiliaries.

CHURCHILL'S SECRET ARMY

ALTHOUGH only ever part of the Home Guard for administrative purposes, one organisation drew on its membership to hand-pick men for its very special duties, and even adopted HG uniforms to cloak its members' occasional appearances while on manoeuvres or during some of its training with other more regular Home Guard units. They were the members of Auxiliary Units, 'Churchill's Secret Army', a top-secret organisation whose members, in the event of invasion, were to go to ground, allow the enemy to pass over and then rise up as a resistance army to harry the army of occupation.

The roots of this organisation can be traced back to 1938, when Royal Engineers Major Laurence Grand set up a secret department in the Foreign Office known as 'Section D' with the specific remit to 'investigate every possibility of attacking potential enemies by means other than the operations of military forces'. Section D forged and maintained a close relationship with another new, and at that time very small, department in the War Office known as GS(R) – General Staff (Research) run by Royal Engineers Major John 'Jo' Holland. In spring 1939 GS(R) was transferred to the Military Intelligence Directorate and re-designated MI(R). Holland was joined by Major Colin McVean Gubbins, a decorated and experienced officer with a particular interest in irregular warfare. He had served with distinction during the First World War and subsequently in both Russia and Ireland. Gubbins compiled three publications for MI(R): *Partisan Leader's Handbook*, *The Art of Guerilla Warfare* and *How to Use High Explosives*. His methods were sneered at by some in the War Office and among the General Staff as 'dirty warfare'. Gubbins preferred that they were quaintly known as 'scallywagging'. In the summer of 1939 he began to approach a few carefully selected British civilians, including explorers, mountaineers and linguists, all of whom might be 'useful' in a time of war.

When war broke out Gubbins was sent on active service missions. In 1940, when he was away in Norway, Whitehall wanted to establish a guerrilla resistance force within Britain in the event of an invasion. With Gubbins away the task was given to Laurence Grand's Section D. Already burdened

Opposite:
Home Guard Soldiers practice close-quarter combat with commando knives at the Commando Training Centre at Achnacarry in the Highlands of Scotland, July 1943. (IWM H 31546)

THE GALE & POLDEN
TRAINING SERIES

FIGHTING PATROL
TACTICS
by COL. G.A.WADE, M.C.
Author of "The Defence of Bloodford Village" etc.

Price 1/6net. by post 1/8

with a heavy workload, Grand organised dumps of explosives and emergency supply stores across the country with a notion that these would be for the use of 'stay behind parties', but no such parties were organised. Upon his return Gubbins was given the task of creating the underground army soon to be known by the deliberately vague title of 'Auxiliary Units' under the aegis of GHQ (General Headquarters) Home Forces, whose C-in-C was Field Marshal 'Tiny' Ironside, to whom Gubbins had served as aide-de-campe at Archangel in 1919. Churchill took a personal interest in the development of these units. A letter to him from the offices of the War Cabinet outlined:

These Auxiliary Units are being formed with two objectives: A) They are intended to provide, within the framework of the Home Guard organisation, small bodies of men especially selected and trained, whose role it will be to act offensively on the flanks and in the rear of any enemy troops who may obtain a foothold in this country. Their action will particularly be directed against tanks and lorries … ammunition dumps, small enemy posts and stragglers.

Issued by the Ministry of Information *in co-operation with the* War Office *and the* Ministry of Home Security

Beating the INVADER

A MESSAGE FROM THE PRIME MINISTER

IF invasion comes, everyone—young or old, men and women—will be eager to play their part worthily. By far the greater part of the country will not be immediately involved. Even along our coasts, the greater part will remain unaffected. But where the enemy lands, or tries to land, there will be most violent fighting. Not only will there be the battles when the enemy tries to come ashore, but afterwards there will fall upon his lodgments very heavy British counter-attacks, and all the time the lodgments will be under the heaviest attack by British bombers. The fewer civilians or non-combatants in these areas, the better—apart from essential workers who must remain. So if you are advised by the authorities to leave the place where you live, it is your duty to go elsewhere when you are told to leave. When the attack begins, it will be too late to go ; and, unless you receive definite instructions to move, your duty then will be to stay where you are. You will have to get into the safest place you can find, and stay there until the battle is over. For all of you then the order and the duty will be : " STAND FIRM ".

This also applies to people inland if any considerable number of parachutists or air-borne troops are landed in their neighbourhood. Above all, they must not cumber the roads. Like their fellow-countrymen on the coasts, they must " STAND FIRM ". The Home Guard, supported by strong mobile columns wherever the enemy's numbers require it, will immediately come to grips with the invaders, and there is little doubt will soon destroy them.

Throughout the rest of the country where there is no fighting going on and no close cannon fire or rifle fire can be heard, everyone will govern his conduct by the second great order and duty, namely, " CARRY ON ". It may easily be some weeks before the invader has been totally destroyed, that is to say, killed or captured to the last man who has landed on our shores. Meanwhile, all work must be continued to the utmost, and no time lost.

The following notes have been prepared to tell everyone in rather more detail what to do, and they should be carefully studied. Each man and woman should think out a clear plan of personal action in accordance with the general scheme

Winston S. Churchill

STAND FIRM

1. What do I do if fighting breaks out in my neighbourhood?

Keep indoors or in your shelter until the battle is over. If you can have a trench ready in your garden or field, so much the better. You may want to use it for protection if your house is damaged. But if you are at work, or if you have special orders, carry on as long as possible and only take cover when danger approaches. If you are on your way to work, finish your journey if you can.

If you see an enemy tank, or a few enemy soldiers, do not assume that the enemy are in control of the area. What you have seen may be a party sent on in advance, or stragglers from the main body who can easily be rounded up

---

Left:
The Battle of Britain was over and Churchill turned up the offensive with 'Beating the Invader' in May 1941.

Below:
Men of 22nd (Stanmore) Battalion, Middlesex Home Guard. Dressed for stalking and raiding with padded boots, blackened faces and balaclavas, they are armed with trench clubs, with two NCOs with Sten guns, as the officer leads them off with his pistol drawn.

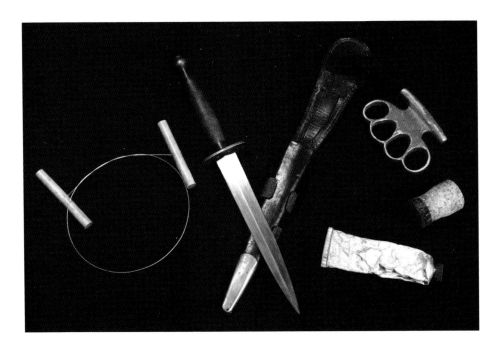

The basic raiding party kit of the auxiliaries — a garrotte, a Fairbairn-Sykes fighting knife, a knuckle duster, a burnt cork for blacking the face and an early tube of camouflage cream made by Colgate, the toothpaste manufacturers. They were also known to carry improvised trench clubs and rubber truncheons.

Their activities will also include sniping. B) The other function of the Auxiliary Units is to provide a system of intelligence whereby Regular Forces in the field can be kept informed of what is happening behind enemy lines.

The letter went on to point out that each unit would comprise no more than a dozen men; they were to be provided with weaponry and equipped with wireless and field telephones apparatus. Each unit was to be accommodated in specially designed camouflaged and concealed (usually underground) operational bases where food, water, weapons and ammunition would be stored. Once training got under way the auxiliaries were also taught how to disrupt enemy railways by blowing up tracks, how to destroy petrol and ammunition dumps and how to immobilise enemy aircraft on occupied airfields.

In practice the objective 'A' Auxiliary Units were to become known as Operational Patrols and were usually comprised of between four and eight men in each unit. Patrols would only operate in an area within 15 miles of their base, and they would have no knowledge of the other units in nearby villages. In the event of a successful invasion and enemy occupation they were not to communicate in any way with army command; they had to be isolated and autonomous until a successful counter-attack was made or they were wiped out. All auxiliaries were warned about their operational life expectancy if there was an invasion — about fifteen days, if they were lucky.

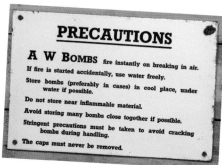

Objective 'B' units became known as Special Duties Section and Signals. These units contained both men and women who were trained to identify vehicles, high-ranking officers and military units, and were to gather intelligence and leave reports in dead letter drops. The reports would be collected by runners and taken to one of over two hundred secret radio transmitters operated by trained civilian signals staff.

Gubbins began his recruitment drive with a team of twelve hand-picked intelligence officers. Every man who was to serve in the Auxiliary Units had to be very carefully selected. The officers and NCO instructors were mostly drawn from the regular army, while the members of the Auxiliary Units were drawn from the Home Guard and a huge variety of backgrounds from civvy street. These ranged from farm labourers, gamekeepers, factory workers, miners and fishermen to clerics, doctors, dentists and local council officials aged from their teens into their seventies. The one common bond was the ability to, above all, keep a secret. Other key factors were that they were resourceful; they could and would, if necessary, blend into the countryside around them; and they were willing to undergo specialist training in guerrilla warfare, quickly become proficient in this and follow orders that they fight to the last round and to the death if need be.

The initial approach to these men was very cloak and dagger. The potential auxiliary would often be called upon by name at his place of work by a well-dressed gentleman claiming to be on 'government business'. Taken to an unmarked car, the true purpose of the visit would be revealed. After a brief explanation of how it was feared that Britain may well be invaded and that an organisation was being set up to 'deal with Germans when they get here', the potential recruit would be told he had been highly recommended and would be asked if he would be prepared to join.

If he agreed, he would be told to report to the post office, Highworth, Wiltshire, where he would present proof of identity to its innocuous-looking postmistress, Mabel Stranks. She would then disappear through a door and upon her return announce, 'Somebody's coming to fetch you.' She would

Above left:
Auxiliaries were trained in a wide variety of explosives and grenades. The Bernards Publishers *Explosives* manual has been found among the effects of many former auxiliaries.

Above:
Notice from the inside of the lid of an Albright and Wilson (AW) bomb box. Not only kept under water and bridges, many of these boxes of bombs were buried by both Home Guard and Auxiliary Units and are still being found today.

carry on about her business and refuse to answer any questions. It was a simple cover but an effective one. Unmarked transport would arrive and take him to nearby Coleshill House – GHQ Auxiliary Units. During the war years about 4,000 auxiliaries were trained in advanced guerrilla warfare, including unarmed combat, assassination, sabotage and demolition at Coleshill. Further training was carried out with predominantly regular army units on military training areas local to the Auxiliary Unit or from group to group by a local instructor.

For most of their existence many Auxiliary Units had no uniforms and performed their duties in their work clothes or perhaps a set of army denims. In 1943 (after a wrangle with the War Office), if auxiliaries did wear uniforms they were allowed to wear the khaki 'Home Guard' title printed with the standard yellow letters. Below that were the county letter designations in which they were based, and below that the number 201, 202 or 203. The number 201 signified Scotland and Northumberland; 202 units ran from Yorkshire and southwards to the line of the Thames and Wales; 203 covered south and south-east commands.

Their equipment was impressive. Initially patrols improvised with cudgels, hunting or sharpened domestic carving knives, knuckle-dusters and cheese-cutting wires to act as garrottes. Soon they were provided with rubber truncheons, quality pistols such as a Smith and Wesson revolver, and a selection of the latest weapons, including a variety of grenades, incendiary devices, a silenced pistol, a magnificent .22 calibre sniper rifle, Thompson sub-machine guns and later Sten guns. They were also issued Fairbairn-Sykes fighting knives, quantities of detonators and plastic explosives. Even today stashes of all the aforementioned weaponry, including plastic explosives, are still being discovered when the cellars and garages of ex-auxiliaries are cleared out.

In total about 7,000 auxiliaries were recruited, trained and established in groups across Britain. It is thought over five hundred Auxiliary Unit operational bases (OBs) were built in secret in local woodland by Royal Engineers; many patrols also had additional concealed observation posts (OPs). Many of the known OBs and OPs have collapsed or flooded over the years, and many still remain

The Countryman's Diary, presented with the compliments of Highworth Fertilisers, looks innocent enough and not out of place among a countryman's papers and books – it was in fact issued to patrol leaders of the Auxiliary Units and gives instructions for the use of all manner of explosive devices and detonators used by 'Churchill's Secret Army'.

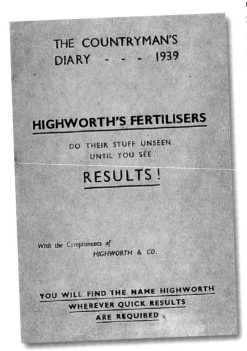

THE COUNTRYMAN'S
DIARY - - - 1939

HIGHWORTH'S FERTILISERS

DO THEIR STUFF UNSEEN
UNTIL YOU SEE

RESULTS !

With the Compliments of
HIGHWORTH & CO.

YOU WILL FIND THE NAME HIGHWORTH
WHEREVER QUICK RESULTS
ARE REQUIRED

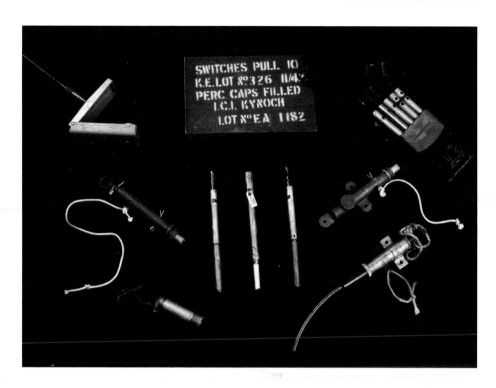

undiscovered. While most of the HG units were stood down in 1944, the Auxiliary Units carried on until 1945. After the war those who had served with Auxiliary Units were sent small lapel badges as a mark of thanks. These badges are in the shape of a shield divided with a red upper and blue lower (reflecting the colours of GHQ Home Forces). The centre is surmounted by a crown; the number 202 is in the middle, with the figure 1 above the zero and the number 3 below.

Above:
A selection of fuses, time pencils and pull switches – all of them tools for 'scallywagging' by the Operational Patrols of the Auxiliary Units.

Far left:
Insignia worn by 202 Battalion Auxiliary Unit members in Suffolk.

Left::
Lapel badge presented to members of Auxiliary Units after their stand down as a small mark of recognition for their services.

THE
LION ROARED
HIS DEFIANCE

THE CALL CAME AND
WAS ANSWERED TO THE FULL
The Home Guard watched & waited
1940-1944

STAND DOWN

A S PROGRESS was made by the Allies from the D-Day landings in June 1944, many HGs could see the reason for a Home Guard diminish, and inevitably the days of the organisation were numbered. On 30 August 1944 the War Office issued 'Instructions for Standing Down the Home Guard'; a formal notice circulated in October gave notification that the Home Guard was to stand down from active duties in November 1944. Parades and march pasts were held to mark the occasion as each battalion stood down. Several of the most senior officers, including Field Marshal Ironside, made personal appearances, received the salutes, led parades and gave one final address. Many of the group photographs that survive of the Home Guard seem to date from this time, as the service stripes, proficiency badges and full uniform turnout of these now smart military units testify. Most battalions and companies held 'stand down' dinners and produced colourful, patriotic and even comic menu cards to mark the occasion.

The Home Guard were allowed to take part in the VE and VJ Victory parades. The War Office announced that the Home Guard would cease to exist from 31 December 1945, but they did parade just one last time when a very proud contingent took part in the Victory Parade through London in June 1946. Certificates of thanks bearing the facsimile signature of King George VI, stating the name and years served, were sent to every HG; many were also entitled to the award of the Defence Medal, the criteria being a minimum of three years' service between June 1940 and November 1944. Tragically, despite answering Britain's call and training harder than any other civilian unit, due to the secret nature of the Auxiliary Units they were unable to claim the Defence Medal. This only changed in 1996, when the Ministry of Defence authorised the award for those men who had served at least three years.

The war had taken its toll on the membership of the Home Guard. Hansard records that on 29 May 1945 Sir George Jones, MP for Stoke Newington, asked what the total number of casualties suffered by the Home Guard was to date. Sir Edward Grigg, the Secretary of State for War, replied

Opposite:
Cover of *The Lion Roared his Defiance*, a tribute to the Home Guard 'compiled by three Home Guard Officers'. It is a very fine example of the many booklets and books written to chart the exploits of particular Home Guard battalions, companies and platoons from across Britain and published in the months and years immediately after the stand down of the Home Guard in 1944.

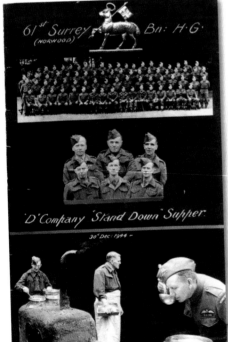

"One who never turned his back but marched breast forward
Never doubted clouds would break."
—Robert Browning.

SOUTHERN GROUP :: A. COMPANY
4TH BATT. WARWICKS. HOME GUARD

Farewell Dinner

SENIOR SCHOOL
BIDFORD-ON-AVON

FRIDAY, DECEMBER 8TH, 1944

In the years when our Country
was in mortal danger

JOHN LAKEY

who served 11th June 1940 - 31st December 1944.

gave generously of his time and
powers to make himself ready
for her defence by force of arms
and with his life if need be.

George R.I.

THE HOME GUARD

Commanding Officers' Certificate

**8TH (CINQUE PORTS) BATTALION
KENT HOME GUARD**

Rank B.Q.M.S.   Name C.W.P. DRAKE

Company 413 Bty. Platoon

You have shown great keenness and have been willing to sacrifice your own personal interests and comforts in order to make yourself efficient to carry out Home Guard duties. By so doing you have assisted in the team work and general efficiency of your Platoon during your period of service with the Home Guard.

Your co-operation and good service has been much appreciated, and if at any time I am called upon to recommend Home Guard personnel for a Good Service Decoration or Certificate, I shall have much pleasure in including your name on my list of recommendations.

Thanking you for your good service to your Country and wishing you all the best in the future.

19, MANOR ROAD
FOLKESTONE.
31st December, 1944.

Lieut. Colonel Commanding,
8th (Cinque Ports) Battalion,
Kent Home Guard.

Opposite top:
Field Marshal Lord Ironside GCB, CMG, CBE, DSO leads the stand down parade of 5th (North Walsham) Battalion, Norfolk Home Guard, 1944. This battalion had companies and platoons in villages spread across a wide area both inland and along the north Norfolk coast. The battalion parade state was seventy-seven officers and 1,724 other ranks.

Opposite bottom left:
Souvenir menu card for the stand down supper for D Company, 61st (Norwood) Battalion, Surrey Home Guard.

Opposite bottom right:
Farewell dinner programme and menu for A Company, 4th Battalion, Warwickshire Home Guard, December 1944. The drinks (recorded in bold on the reverse) were 'Beer, Beer and More Beer!'

Above left:
The Service Certificate sent after the stand down to all who had served in the Home Guard.

Above right:
Commanding Officer's Certificate of Appreciation presented on the stand down to Battery Quarter Master Sergeant Cecil Drake, 413 Battery, 8th (Cinque Ports) Battalion, Kent Home Guard.

Right:
The Defence Medal, awarded to all Home Guard who served a minimum of three years between June 1940 and November 1944.

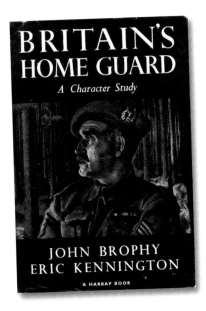

that 438 members of the Home Guard were killed or died of wounds, and 557 were wounded as a result of enemy action. In addition, 768 died as a result of other casualties attributable to service, and 5,633 had been admitted to hospital.

In the immediate aftermath of the war ex-Home Guardsmen gathered to help write up their unit histories, and several established rifle clubs to 'keep their eye in' and stay in contact with their pals. John Brophy had put pen to paper for his final book about the Home Guard in 1945. This was no training manual but an eloquent study of the men themselves with evocative colour portraits by official war artist Eric Kennington. Both Brophy and every HG history since have spoken of good fellowship, not naively believing some utopia was achieved but reflecting on the beers shared after training exercises, intimate talks about anything and everything on lonely night guards and the long-awaited dawn in a sky dark with smoke and reddened with flames from the fires of the previous night's blitz. Brophy concluded with a tribute to the men of the Home Guard:

Above:
Britain's Home Guard: A Character Study (1945). Superbly illustrated with paintings by Eric Kennington, this book was John Brophy's final tribute to the Home Guard.

> Some have rows of medal ribbons; some have none. Some are grey haired: some still have the flush of youth in their cheeks. What they hold in common is not readily identified. You can call it self-reliance, if you wish, or self-respect or resolution, or merely patience … Whatever it is, this elusive quality of character, it enabled nearly two million Home Guards for

A variety of lapel badges worn by Home Guard when in mufti – for recognition as HG members during the war and as 'old comrades' badges in the years after.

four and a half years of the most terrible war in history, to continue their duties unremittingly, as members of an organised community. They gave to that community and took from it, and yet each remains himself, recognisable at sight, not as a type, a standardised product, but an individual. And that, I feel, has something to do with what we are getting at when we talk about democracy.

The return of a Conservative government headed by Winston Churchill in 1951 saw a brief revival of the Home Guard. Volunteers, both men and women aged between eighteen and sixty-five, were asked to sign on for two years and to undertake a minimum of fifteen hours' training every three months. Up-to-date uniforms with black berets and county regiment cap badges were provided; Home Guard insignia of white lettering and numbers on a scarlet background were emblazoned on the battledress. The problem was that despite the Suez Crisis that was making the country think back to protecting British interests abroad, there was no direct threat to Britain – no invasion force was poised just over the channel – and thus recruitment was painfully slow. By 1952 the total national strength of the new Home Guard was just 28,000, and it never surpassed 37,000. The organisation limped on until 1956 and, with the reorganisation of the army, was formally disbanded in 1957.

The champion shooting team of 55th (Sutton & Cheam) Battalion, Surrey Home Guard, 1944. After stand down many HG units established their own rifle clubs that lasted long after the war.

The Home Guard necktie – available from good military tailors from December 1940.

Advance and be recognized

with the original Home Guard Tie, worn by many thousands of Home Guards. To avoid confusion, be sure the tie you buy has these colours. Make a note of them now.

Navy
Light Blue
Maroon
Green

ASK FOR (AND BE SURE YOU GET) THE ORIGINAL

Home Guard Tie
Registered No. 398516

OBTAINABLE FROM OUTFITTERS IN YOUR ZONE
Also Blazers and Mufflers

Another citizen army akin to that of the British Home Guard in the Second World War was not to be and has never been seen since. Undoubtedly the memory of the Home Guard will be kept alive for generations to come by David Croft and Jimmy Perry's comedy series *Dad's Army*, based directly on co-writer and creator Jimmy Perry's real-life experiences in the Local Defence Volunteers. Perry was just fifteen when he joined the 10th Hertfordshire Battalion, with a mother who did not like him being out at night and who worried he might catch cold – he was the real Pike. All the characters in the series could be found to a greater or lesser extent in every HG platoon. Those who served in the original LDV and HG found touchstones in the stories told in the eighty-four episodes, screened initially between 1968 and 1977. It serves as a reminder to viewers today of the determined men who answered Britain's call in its darkest hours in 1940, those who served in the real 'Dad's Army' – the Home Guard.

One last picture, for the record – a group of Suffolk Home Guard officers and sergeants shortly before stand down, 1944.

SUGGESTED READING

Angell, Stewart. *The Secret Sussex Resistance 1940–1944*. Middleton Press, 1996.

Anon. *The Lion Roared His Defiance*. Marten & Son, 1944.

Brophy, John. *Britain's Home Guard: A Character Study*. Harrap, 1945.

Carroll, David. *The Home Guard*. Sutton, 1999.

Carroll, David. *Dad's Army: The Home Guard 1940–44*. Sutton, 2002.

Fine, Captain Simon. *With the Home Guard*. Alliance Press, 1943.

General Staff. *Notes on the German Preparations for Invasion of the United Kingdom*. Naval & Military Press (originally published 1942; reprinted 2004).

Graves, Charles. *The Home Guard of Britain*. Hutchinson, 1943.

Hoare, Adrian. *Standing Up to Hitler: The Story of Norfolk's Home Guard and 'Secret Army' 1940–44*. Countryside Books, 2002.

Longmate, Norman. *The Real Dad's Army*. Hutchinson, 1974.

Longmate, Norman. *If Britain had Fallen*. Greenhill, 2004.

Lampe, David. *The Last Ditch*. Cassell, 1968.

Mackenzie, S. P. *The Home Guard*. Oxford University Press, 1996.

Mills, Jon and Terry Carney. *In the Space of a Single Day: The Insignia and Uniforms of the LDV and Home Guard 1940–1944 and 1952–1956*. Wardens Publishing, 2001.

Osborne, Mike. *Pillboxes of Britain and Ireland*. Tempus, 2007.

Oxenden, Major N. V. *Auxiliary Units History and Achievements 1940–1944*. BRO Museum, 1998.

Radnor, John. *It All Happened Before: The Home Guard Through the Ages*. Harrap, 1945.

Schellenberg, Walter and John Erickson. *Invasion 1940: The Nazi Invasion Plan for Britain*. St Ermin's, 2000.

Shaw, Frank and Joan. *We Remember the Home Guard*. Shaw, 1990.

Slater, Hugh. *Home Guard for Victory*. Victor Gollancz, 1941.

Storey, Neil. *Norfolk at War*. Sutton, 2001.

Street, A. G. *From Dusk Till Dawn*. Blandford Press, 1945.

Warwicker, John. *Churchill's Underground Army*. Frontline Books, 2009.

Warwicker, John (ed.). *With Britain in Mortal Danger*. Cerberus, 2004.

Whittaker, L. B. *Stand Down*. Westlake, 1990.

INDEX

Page numbers in italics refer to illustrations.